"A Sol

and a Marine

Walked into this War…"

John T. Reardon

"A Soldier, a Sailor and a Marine Walked into this War…"

PREFACE

This writer has previously paid tribute to the veterans of the Civil War, WW II, and Vietnam, by compiling their first person stories, received in various formats, into a more permanent booklet format. In response to that attempt to honor their memory by preserving their individual accounts, many readers continue to come forward with additional first person accounts, often informal, brief or in manuscript form.

So the tribute by preservation continues, and with great respect to these veterans, and to the entire "Greatest Generation," these accounts are compiled and shared at this time.

ACKNOWLEDGEMENTS

I would like to thank the veterans who lived and then recorded these stories. I am grateful for their permission to include their stories in this work. The stories are presented here as closely as possible to the form in which they were given to me. Each also contributed photos or sketches. I humbly pass them along in tribute to their service.

I would also like to thank my editors and proof readers, and my patient and loving wife, Sally.

The various pictures are either from public domain sources or have been provided by the respective contributors.

the long line of tanks and halftracks behind you, creeping ominously along thru the blackness, blackout lights just visible. Every now and then you heard the angry bowel of a 500 horse tank engine as the driver shifted for a bad stretch of the road.

The bivouac party had gone ahead. It found a big house for the Bn CP and had gone down the streets, knocking at each door and asking for rooms. They found places for all the men to sleep in, in these Alsacian houses, and courtyards in which to park the vehicles.

We moved in before dawn, the sky a faint gray instead of black and the stucco and timber farm houses of the village huddled together like gray stone sheep with slanted red tile roofs, just under a ridge of land and around a bend in the road.

The bivouac party was waiting for us. The Bn CP and the houses where we were to live; but the tanks stayed on the streets because we were to start the attack at 0530. And we could here the whine and the empty whoom of incoming mail somewhere close enough.

It was simple. To defend, we were to attack Hatten with the Infantry and drive the enemy out. The Infantry would pass thru us and take up defensive positions on the high ground beyond the town.

In the CP, the Col. was bending over the situation map with the staff. Hatten was due east of us then. A single track French railway ran east and west, passed a few hundred yards south of Hatten and continued on east. Halfway between us and Hatten, also north of us, lay the town of Rittershoffen. Another unit was to clean out Rittershoffen! We were to pass to the south of Rittershoffen, along the railroad; we were to swing north and drive into Hatten. An Infantry BN was to be with us; the infantry was to be to the south of the railroad and we to the north.

The Kraut could see us from the high ground north of Hatten. For the land slopes gently up from the north edge of the Hagenau forest to the crest above the Seltzbach river. And it was on that crest that the Kraut had set up his observation post. Hatten is about half way up that gentle slope.

From the east end of Rittershoffen, you could see into Hatten, and you could fire into Hatten. And the Kraut held the east end of Rittershoffen-- with infantry and two captured American 57mm anti tank guns.

Capt. Persky, of St Paul Minn. commanded Co C. At least, he did command it that morning. He was to be the attack Co., and one of his platoons, commanded by Lt. Seth

Sprague, of Hingham, Mass. was to be attached to the infantry bn. moving south of the railroad. At least, Lt. Sprague was in command of the platoon that morning. Or what was then the platoon.

Co A commanded by Capt Tharp of Macon Ga was in support. So were the assault guns commanded by Lt R. Harper of Auburn Neb. Reserve Co was commanded by Capt B Tilden of Weymouth, Mass.

Let us follow Lt Sprague. As the eastern sky turned to lighter gray, directly ahead of him, his tanks are are standing in the narrow frozen street of a small Alsacian. town. Beside him rise the steep roofed plaster and timber houses, black in the early morning. The engine of his tank is idling easily and he is standing at,the turret, hatch open, muffled in his combat suit and scarf. It is Cold!

His radio is crackling softly and the yellow warming light flashes on and he hears his call word crackling, "Move out! Move Out!" "Willco," he says and switched to interphone. "Move out, Move Out" he says to the driver.

The tank engine roars suddenly in his ears and he does not hear the driver shift into gear. The tank lurches a little and pulls a little ahead. He feels its familiar grating progress of the steel tracks claw at the ice-hard roads. The engine roars again and the driver shifts to third. Sprague's head is even with the windows of the houses and he can see the road better before him.

Presently he is out of town and following the road by the ghostly white fields. On both sides of the road are lines of trees: poplar and sycamore, as there always are in this country. Now he is watching for the cross road, his line of departure. There is a frosty mist in the air.

He finds the cross road. It is 0803. "Crossed line one," he says, and a voice answers: "Roger." He continues on, slowly. It will be a gray, cold, miserable day. The mist is falling on the fields, freezing on the ground. It is turning the trees of the black woods to his south a perfect white. By 0850 he has moved 800 yards. Passed phase line two.

At 0913. "Heavy enemy artillery fire" he says. "Heavy enemy artillery fire."
"Where is it?"
"Don't know," he says. "Can't see. Visibility poor. All I know is it's coming in."

The enemy is on the high ground to his left; they are behind him now, in Rittershoffen. He is in his tank, the engine roaring hot behind him, creaking and jolting over the frozen ground. His turret hatch is closed now. He cannot see the infantry, but he can hear the high-pitched scream of the artillery, right on him; and he can see the craters suddenly appear in the frozen ground ahead of him. He can feel the lift of the tank sometimes as one hits close. And he can hear the shrapnel smash angrily at the armor sides.

He is headed northeast, directly toward Hatten. He is within anti¬tank gun range but he cannot see any anti-tank guns. He can make out the houses in Hatten, the slanted roofs, white from mist – a small farming village, lying on the slope above him.

At 0930. Capt. Persky is on the air.

"Can't contact Sprague," he says. "I've lost two tanks out of the platoon." Later it turns out to be three, and fourteen men.

Lt. Francis E. Marshall of Mt. Pleasant, Pennsylvania, Company A, is dispatched to go into town to assist the infantry. He goes east; then north. All this while the bitter fighting is going on. By now, it is plain where the anti-tank guns are firing from: from the south edge of Hatten, and from much farther east, so that when Marshall turns north these anti-tank guns are on his right flank.

The American artillery is not quiet. As Marshall reports the locations of the guns, battalion after battalion sends out its roaring volleys from far back. Marshall can see the bursts of their hits. Again and again, it seems the guns are knocked out, but either the Germans send up new crews, or they send up new guns, for presently the anti-tank guns start firing again.

And all along to the east the burp guns are firing on the infantry; and the Kraut artillery comes in again and again; and the mortars fall almost without stopping; and men are hit, and men are blown apart, and men lie on the frozen ground in helpless fear, and hear the mortars coming in. And half laugh when they miss.

So it is not enough to say that Lt. Marshall got three of his tanks into the western edge of Hatten; that he went too far east and had to come back; that he took up a firing position.

It took him all afternoon. And all afternoon there was fighting; and all day there was dying; and it is not possible to tell everything that happened. There was a battalion of infantry in there, to mention just one unit; and each of the men of that battalion could tell you his own story--and a different one--and each man was afraid in his own way, and brave in his own way, or cowardly in his own way. Lt.

stated that more than a hundred men in his unit were killed in a single day.

The tenseness and fighting went on. The artillery still came in its endless scream and whoomp. And the small arms chattered endlessly; and the Krauts were in the next houses.

You would be on one side of a wall and the Krauts on the other; and you would try to lob hand grenades over to get them; and the infantry would set up a mortar and take off all the increments except one and try to lob shells over one house onto the next. And the dead lying in the streets began to get on your nerves, and the tenseness of always looking down the sights, always waiting; and the artillery was always coming and you knew it was only a question of time before one landed on the house you were in. The fighting had reached such vicious pitch that they tried to range in eight inch howitzers on a single house, which is something like trying to hit a fly with a shotgun.

The fighting went on and on. That next day and the next day and the next day and the next day and the next day and the next.

"Counterattacks were beaten off in the Hatten area today," was the way news dispatches read. But that did not tell of the artillery fire and what a counterattack was. That did not tell you of the infantry staff sergeant (best dammed platoon leader in the Army) in combat for months, scheduled to get to the rear at 1930 to take a physical to become a second lieutenant, and how he was killed at 1530. That did not tell you of the death and screaming, the sweating in that ice cold air and the suffering.

It did not tell of the hours on hours of endless waiting while nothing happened--hours two hundred minutes long, and days and nights two hundred hours, waiting, till finally you wanted something to happen.

These men could tell you--or let the official words of their citations tell you:

"Sgt. William T. Summers of Schnectady, New York, Company C, on the 18th of January at Hatten, France, at about 1400 was maneuvering his tank to get out of range of an anti-tank gun. While so engaged he saw a light tank get hit and start to burn. Summers at once went to the light tank's aid. Upon arriving he dismounted and helped evacuate the crew. The driver of the burning tank was hurt and needed first aid. Summers gave him the necessary treatment, mounted the wounded men on the back deck of his tank and rode away with them. During this entire time Sgt. Summers was entirely exposed to small arms and mortar fire falling in heavy concentrations."

"On the night of the 13th of January at Hatten, France, platoon leader, Lieutenant --- was wounded. S/Sgt. Pennington P. Smith of Shreveport, Louisiana, and Pfc. James Barbara of Brooklyn, New York, both of Company A, dismounted from their tank into intense enemy fire and shielded the body of the Lieutenant with their own bodies, while S/Sgt. Smith administered first aid. When it was necessary for someone to ride the back deck of the tank to give the officer protection and keep him from falling off, Pfc. Barbara volunteered. Pfc. Barbara not only kept up the first aid treatment necessary on the trip, but shielded the officer with his own body against intense small arms, mortar, and artillery fire; and the Lieutenant was successfully evacuated. S/Sgt. Smith returned to his platoon and assumed command, reorganized it and made a personal foot reconnaissance to discover the best route for his tanks. In the course of his reconnaissance he directed the evacuation of an infantry platoon sergeant. All this accomplished under intense small arms and mortar fire. The success of the mission was largely due to the cool leadership of S/Sgt. Smith."

"On the 17th of January, at Hatten France, Tech 4 John Pitcher, of Altoona, Pennsylvania, and Pfc. Richard L. Duvall of McBain, Michigan both of Company D, were members of the crew of a light tank that was hit by an 88mm gun. The tank burst into flames. Under small arms fire Tech 4 Pitcher and Pfc. Duvall had dismounted from the flaming tank. When they saw the other two members of the crew did not come out, the two men returned to the tank and pulled the wounded gunner, who was aflame, from the tank. Pfc. Duvall rolled the burning body on the ground and laid on the blazing clothes to extinguish the flame. They could not evacuate the fourth man. Successful in putting out the fire, the men hailed a passing medium tank and placed the gunner on the rear deck and then laid with him under small arms fire until the safety of an aid station was reached. The gunner has a fifty-fifty chance to live as a result of their action. These men showed unusual courage in the face of great personal danger in helping their comrades in arms.

These are the stories of three men. But they are not enough. Lt. Earl A. Allgrim of Buffalo, New York and S/Sgt. William E. Fadda of San Leandro, California, both of headquarters Company, could tell you how they went out onto the battlefield under heavy artillery and small arms fire to evacuate a tank.

Sgt. Stephen B.Ratchuck, Jr. of Buffalo, New York and Tec 4 Edgar Mongo of Utica, New York both of Company B, could tell you how they walked on foot through artillery fire again and again to fix tank radios.

Lt. Eugene O. Marsack of Grosspoint, Michigan, and Pvt. Henry J. Erickson of Brooklyn, New York, both of Company D, could tell you how on the night of the 17th of January, the Krauts hit a half-track loaded with wounded men, and how they dismounted from their tank in all that fire and hitched the half-track to the tank and towed it to safety.

These are the stories of six more men. But the story is not told. There are thousands of stories. A story for every man. And some of the men are living. And some of them are dead. And perhaps not even all those stories would tell the story of Hatten.

The battle went on.

That day and the next day and the next day and the next day and the next.

Company B came up from Drusenheim, short of tanks from its last fight. Capt. Thomas C. Beaty of Wichita Falls, Texas, in command. This was on the 15th, and that night Lt. John L. Perkins of Amsterdam, New York, was killed outside his tank at Hatten. We found a letter he had written to his wife, in pencil, and not mailed. So we stamped it and sent it out.

Lt. Cullis V. Sears of Lumber City, Georgia, went into that town that night.

By the 17th, Company A was sent back to Durrenbach. Capt. Tharpe had been wounded; and Lt..Rael was back in the hospital. Company B, low on tanks to start, had lost Lt. Perkins.

Company C was low on tanks. Capt. Persky, wounded; Lt. Hilbert C. Jones of Elcho, Wisconsin, wounded. Lt. Sprague, missing; Lt. Sidney Hack of Brooklyn, New York, wounded. Company C had one officer left.

The Germans still held Hatten, though.

If you went up to the gentle rolling field south of Hatten, you could see the burned hulls of American tanks scattered there. You could see the German tanks there, too; and if you wanted to fight your way into the streets of Hatten, you could see more burned out wrecks there. American and German.

The Seventh Army decided to pull back. It was only a short distance, but the papers told how the seventh had out-foxed von Rundstedt; how it had fought and fought and fought his counterattacks until the very last second; and then when he put all his weight behind his final punch, the

Seventh had pulled back, and he was swinging at air, and the Seventh was waiting for him again as he stumbled off his balance.

We moved out on the 20th.

We moved back, to the south and west, and left Hatten behind us. We moved out in the night, and the tanks stayed to cover the infantry; and the line of the battalion--not as long now, crawled slowly down the black roads.

Behind was Hatten, and behind was the fighting. Behind were the endless artillery barrages and the waiting. Behind were the fires and the dead.

Behind was the broken German offensive.

Behind was the broken German offensive.

Bob Clancy

Navy Seabee

Bob Clancy

1941

The hostile news emanating from Europe was of grave concern. The belligerent nature of Adolph Hitler's aggression strongly challenged the United States neutrality. Because of this concern, the government started to draft men who were twenty-one years and older. On December 7, 1941, all prior speculation about our neutrality turned to reality when Japan bombed Pearl Harbor. On the following day, after President Roosevelt addressed Congress, war was declared on Japan, Germany and Italy. This declaration of war occurred sixteen days prior to my seventeenth birthday. I was enjoying a quiet Sunday afternoon with my friends, Harold Clyde and John Dunnigan, when we heard about Pearl Harbor being bombed. Spontaneously, we began to speculate the possible impact it would have on us, three high school students. Although I was only seventeen, I understood this news was a sign that the life I was living was about to change, and if it was, I wanted it to be of my choosing and not by chance. As the war intensified, Congress debated lowering the draft age from twenty one to eighteen years.

Being on the brink of turning eighteen, and wanting no part of the Army, I did a lot of serious thinking, and what I was thinking would ultimately require my parents' consent.. By this time, my Logan Avenue friends began to enlist in the services, Bob Scully and Joe McRea enlisted in the Marine Corps. Eddie Schields enlisted in the Navy, my brother Frank was drafted in the Army Medical Corps and my cousin, Buster, enlisted in the Navy.

During World War II, it was customary for families with active duty servicemen to hang a banner in their front window, denoting with stars, the number of family members serving in the armed forces. Mom proudly displayed her single star flag and I knew she was not looking to add another star.

1942

As Congress debated lowering the draft age to 18 years, I began to request my parents to let me join the Navy. Being 17 required parental consent. I understood their reluctance, as my brother Frank was already on active duty in the Army. It was only after my parents learned that I might lose my enlistment option that they consented to my enlistment. It was Dec 14, 1942, ten days prior to my 18th birthday. I lost no time enlisting in the United States Navy

Seabees, and was subsequently inducted into active duty service on January 27, 1943.

Prior to the time of my enlistment, I was a senior at Christopher Columbus High School and residing with my parents and siblings at 271 Logan Avenue, The Bronx, New York. It was my "Home Town." Logan Avenue, which became my springboard of life, from high school student and civilian to the United States Navy and many other phases of later life. My mother subsequently received my high school diploma while I was stationed on Guadalcanal in the South Pacific.

1943

Leaving home for the first time at 18 was an emotional experience I wasn't quite prepared for, especially being aware of my mother's concern for my brother Frank. And now my leaving for the Navy, added to that concern. The predawn morning I left home was a dreary, cold, rainy February day. While walking alone to the local bus stop I waved back to Mom for the last time. She stretched out the apartment window to respond back with a faint wave. I feel certain it wasn't long after she proudly added the second star to the service banner.

The Navy induction center, located in lower Manhattan,

was swarming with enlistees, and like myself, they were mostly teenagers. From there we were bussed to Penn Station and boarded an overnight train to Richmond, Virginia. It was here I had my first Navy breakfast of hominy grits, fried apples and sausage. I figured it had to get better. After chow, a new name for food, we continued to our final destination, Camp Perry, a Sea Bee boot camp in Williamsburg, Virginia. Shortly after arriving, my high school hang-up about being naked in the school locker room was completely stripped of me, along with my still soaking wet clothes. In a state of complete nakedness, along with dozens of other boots, I was physically examined, inoculated, against who knows what, and issued my uniform (thank God, clothes at last.)

After dressing for the first time as a sailor I was rushed to a barber for a quick buzz cut before posing for my photo ID. All of this transitional exercise, from civilian to sailor, was completed in a brief time frame. (The soaking wet clothes were boxed and sent home, where they arrived frozen solid.) Despite the frenzy of it, I was content with my decision to join the Navy and the responsibilities associated with this new life.

After six weeks of intensive training to be a land based sailor, I was transferred from the snow free environment of

Virginia to Camp Endicott, Rhode Island, where the snow is knee deep all winter. It was here I was assigned to the 82nd Construction Battalion, for the duration of my Navy career. While at this base I earned my first liberty, and it was my first time off base in dress uniform. At first it was a strange feeling until it became obvious that there were more people in Navy uniforms than there were civilians.

This was also my first experience to legally enter a bar room. Being a novice, and wanting to avoid looking like a "hayseed" from Throngs Neck, I ordered a rum and coke, one of the more popular drinks of the time. It tasted as unappetizing as my first cigarette, and like cigarettes, I haven't had one since all though I still enjoy listening to the Andrew Sisters musical version of "Rum and Coca Cola," which was a wartime favorite .

Soon after the battalion was fully complemented, it was transferred to Gulfport, Mississippi. The Navy always went first class when relocating personnel. In this case, we enjoyed Pullman Cars for sleeping and enjoyed waiter service in the dining car. Upon arriving in Gulfport, on April 1, 1943, in ninety-degree weather, in winter uniforms, the battalion was granted a ten day embarkation leave. It was advised that we enjoy this time with our families as it would be the final opportunity until after the war. Unlike the comfortable Navy sponsored trip south, the trip home was in a vintage overcrowded coach, where you either had to stand or convert your sea bag into a seat. In view of the fact it was our first trip home since being inducted, it was tolerated in good spirit. After arriving back in Gulfport, with memories of the leave still very much with us, advanced training intensified under Marine drill instructors.

The near tropic heat we were experiencing was an omen as to where the battalion was destined. It didn't appear to be Alaska. After completing a strenuous training period, the battalion moved to Port Hueneme, Oxnard, California, a major Sea Bee embarkation base. Oxnard was a frontier type town, cluttered with bars, eateries, souvenir shops and other activities sailors like to shop for. It was the local watering hole for evening liberties. However, a weekend pass provided the opportunity to visit Hollywood or Los Angeles, seventy-five miles from base. These attractive, military friendly cities, were the ultimate destinations and were easily accessible by hitchhiking. They both provided superior U. S. O. facilities, some of which were staffed by Hollywood celebrities. I was fortunate to enjoy visiting both these cities on several occasions before all liberties came to an abrupt end in July 1943, when the battalion was restricted to base.

Port Hueneme wasn't all fun and liberty. The battalion was introduced to a new phase of training - amphibious landing craft exercises. This became a daily routine for the remainder of time at base. Concurrent with this training a cargo ship was loading the heavy construction equipment and supplies to support our mission that remained secret.

Embarkation

On July 10, 1943, bulldozers, graders, trucks, jeeps, air compressors, gasoline and necessary parts and supplies were loaded aboard the Cape San Martin. Battalion personnel and support requirements were stowed aboard the M.S. Island Mail. At sunset, both ships sailed from Port Hueneme for a destination that still remained unidentified. Later in the day, the Commander, Tom Fowler, announced that our destination was Noumea, New Caledonia, a French island possession in the South Pacific. He added, the voyage would take approximately eighteen days and we would be sailing without a Navy escort. Our immediate reaction was not so much about the destination as it was about sailing in hostile waters for eighteen days without an armed escort.

Shipboard life was an adventure in itself as the vessel

zigzagged across the blue Pacific. The erratic course was intended as an anti-submarine maneuver employed by unarmed ships sailing without armed escorts. There were severe restrictions about throwing debris overboard that could possibly become a telltale sign for submarines indicating the ship's presence.

Shipboard trash was dumped overboard after dark, following which the ship changed course and always sailed under mandatory blackout conditions. No lights, matches or smoking were permitted above deck after dark. For entertainment the battalion band played on the aft-deck under a sky that radiated with millions of stars. This majestic sight made me conscious of how inconspicuous we humans are in relation to the universe. The deck space used by the band at night became the chapel area the next morning for daily mass. On Sundays, the Catholic chaplain also conducted nondenominational services for men of other faiths.

Most of the daylight hours were spent above deck reading, playing cards or cribbage, or just ocean watching. Occasionally a whale would be spotted, but you could always count on seeing schools of flying fish and dolphins. Breakfast and dinner were the only meals served, lunch consisted of an apple or orange issued at breakfast. Except to sleep, I seldom ventured below deck during the day.

Since the ship was originally a cargo vessel, the below deck areas were not comfortably suited for living or sleeping. They were extremely cramped, and lacked adequate ventilation that contributed to a hot, stagnant and humid environment.

The showers that were on deck consisted of an open ended steel compartment with several dozen showerheads that continually spouted ocean water, there was no faucets. Each man was issued a bar of brown salt-water soap, which reminded me of a laundry item rather than something for the shower. The soap didn't make a lather and after showering with it there was only a slight feeling of cleanliness and a far less feeling of being refreshed. Like the shower, the head (toilet), was also on deck and of the same design. The head could accommodate a dozen or so men at any one time. The seat consisted of two wood slats that spanned across a narrow steel trough of flowing ocean water. The lack of privacy partitions afforded a communal meeting place to chat with your shipmates about the latest shipboard rumors while doing your thing. It was best to avoid the facility in rough weather as the contents in the trough had a tendency to pitch and roll with the vessel, a spill could easily wind up where least desired.

On July 18, 1943, a major event occurred when the ship crossed the equator. In celebration of the occasion, members of the ship's crew, known as Shellbacks, since they previously crossed the equator, staged an elaborate induction ceremony for those who never crossed, who were known as Pollywogs. In accordance with Navy tradition, the Shellbacks were responsible to induct all Pollywogs into King Neptune's, Ocean Kingdom, and forever bestow upon them the noble title of Shellback. The ceremony was more or less a rogue type of collegiate hazing ceremony, taken by most in good humor. Others found it abusive. Following the induction, cake and cookies, especially prepared for this momentous occasion were served to the newly baptized Shellbacks by the ship's crew. Crossing this imaginary line, dividing the hemispheres, meant we were about half way to New Caledonia.

On the eighteenth day of the voyage, and through early morning haze, a faint outline appeared on the horizon that appeared to be land. It was July 28, 1943. The sighting was officially confirmed, and shortly after New Caledonia appeared in the distance. On approaching the harbor entrance, the ship drifted ever so slowly through open anti-submarine nets into the protected harbor of Noumea, the capital of New Caledonia. The ship dropped anchor eighteen days after we left California, and it was then an emotional sentiment of gratitude was silently expressed that we arrived safely.

New Caledonia

During the following days we participated in various work details in the harbor, mostly aboard floating dry docks. It was a welcomed relief to get off the M.S. Island Mail, now caustically called the "Island Jail", and to be physically active again. The dry dock job entailed cleaning the dock area after a repaired vessel left. Then we'd ready the space for another ship. It was all bull work, and most of the time meant wallowing in heavy deposits of bunker oil and globular clusters of grease. However, the after work benefits more than offset this difficult work. The massive dock was like a floating hotel compared to our ship. It had fresh, hot water showers, real soap that lathered, and an air-conditioned mess hall that served excellent chow.

During our layover we had liberty in Noumea, which was my first experience on foreign soil dealing with a language other than English. The soil was no different than home, however, the language was a challenge. New Caledonia, was a French penal colony, and remains a French possession, speaking the mother tongue. Since the merchants were eager for the U. S. dollar they quickly acquired sufficient English to successfully transact a sale.

Being a port city it was a typical sailor town with many bars, brothels and souvenir shops interspersed with fine, French pastry shops and restaurants. Noumea also provided an opportunity to meet service men from Australia and New Zealand who were much like ourselves and staunch friends of the United States.

Guadalcanal

On August 15, 1943, eighteen days after arriving in New Caledonia, the Island Mail, the Cape San Martin and other United States vessels sailed from Noumea, in convoy formation to the Solomon Islands. Four days later we arrived at Guadalcanal, which was our first war zone base. It was on this island the United States took the initiative and reversed the Japanese expansion in the South Pacific, the success of which was costly to both sides. Remnants of any Japanese presence were limited to occasional night bombings and sniper fire. And "Washing Machine Charlie" would pay harassment visits. (A relatively harmless plane, but loud and annoying.) These actions were more psychological in nature than offensive. The intent was to keep us awake and in wet bunkers all night instead of the comfort of a dry bed.

The most aggressive enemy at this point was the hostile environment and the never-ending challenge to compete with it. Combating the effects of extreme heat, tropical humidity, daily rain showers, insects of all description and trudging through knee-deep mud made for an exhausting day. It was an absolute necessity to sleep within a mosquito net and to medicate daily with atabrine tablets. Both were preventive measures against malaria. Because of the tropical humidity, body fungus was a blight that affected most of us. Our tents were pitched under a canopy of palm and mahogany trees with a dense jungle surrounding the entire camp area. The density of heavy foliage prevented direct sunlight to reach the camp site creating relentless mildew on our clothing as well as it being the principal cause of fungus infections we called jungle rot. The fresh water river flowing through the camp was used for personal bathing and laundry purposes. The Coral Sea was just yards away, where we went swimming and shelling in the small coves along the coastline.

As time passed, living conditions improved. Tents were wired for lights, palm trees were sawed into planking for tent floors and roads were surfaced with crushed coral substantially reducing the mud problem. The Palmolive Company's precious groves of palm trees were leveled by "daisy cutters," to eliminate sniper nests, (and later to provide planking for every tent.) A newly constructed screened in mess hall provided a dry and insect free eating environment. This was the most appreciated improvement, being able to eat without having swarms of flies competing for your chow.

Our primary mission included a variety of assignments. The most critical was resurfacing Henderson Field. This was the principal airstrip the Marine fighter-bombers used in their missions against Japanese targets in the lower Solomon Islands. Rebuilding roads and unloading equipment and supplies from the frequently arriving cargo vessels was another high priority. I was assigned to the stevedore gang responsible for unloading these ships for the duration of our time on Guadalcanal.

Among the extraordinary memories I have of the island was watching the natives enjoying their first taste of ice cream made by the kitchen staff, meeting a French priest who was a former Japanese prisoner and to socialize with the New Zealanders camped next to us. It was always entertaining to watch young native boys scurry up palm trees harvesting coconuts. The few coins they earned were tucked in their ears freeing both hands for the next climb. These unusual experiences were far too extraordinary and unique to be easily forgotten.

The Solomons

It was September 19, 1943, when the battalion pulled stakes and left Guadalcanal for what was to be a twelve month assignment in the Solomon Islands. As the war progressed northward so did the battalion. During this tour the battalion was responsible to build roads, aviation fuel storage tanks, landing strips for Marine P -38 fighters, Quonset huts for command centers, warehouses and an asphalt making plant. In addition to Guadalcanal the 82nd Battalion left its "Can Do" mark on, Munda, Ondonga and Sterling islands.

Second from left, on Stirling Island

1944

1st Row Left to Right — Stirling Island

Red Butler — Texas
yours truly —
Joe Decansky — Penna.
George Booka — Penna.

2 row

Jim Taylor — Mass.
Johnny Murphy — N.Y. State

When approaching the islands from aboard ship they project an illusion of being serene tropical paradises. It was only after going ashore that reality set in, revealing their true deceptiveness. They were hostile, uninviting and challenging and perhaps for these reasons they were mostly uninhabited.

Once ashore you encountered rain forests, massive bogs of mud capable of disabling anything with wheels or tracks, and a personal challenge to walk without losing a boot. Compounding these difficulties was the infinite number of flying and crawling insects, chronic dysentery and body fungus, possibly being beset by all at the same time. While on the islands of Ondonga and Munda, these health concerns were in addition to the unsettling fact the Japanese were shelling us from their stronghold on Kolobangara, an island across a strait from ours. This frequently required spending time in a dark, insect infested underground bunker, with rain water dripping from the overhead. It was not a relaxing end to a day working in 100 degree heat.

Sterling Island, which was almost desert like compared to the others, was our last assignment in the Solomon's. Our campsite was on the beach and at certain times of the month it was not unusual to find the area inundated with land crabs crawling from the jungle to lay their eggs at the waters edge. My first sighting of this massive swarm of purplish-black crabs was startling, watching them slowly crawl to the water. It appeared as if the entire beach was sliding into the sea. It was even more startling to see them crawling through our tent and become tangled in mosquito netting, helmet liners and trapped in our shoes. The density of crabs on the airstrip grounded all flights until after they could be removed. The surviving crabs returned to their jungle habitat to await another signal from mother nature to resume their creepy biological urge to procreate.

As the Solomon Island operation was beginning to phase out, rumors were rampant about the next assignment. Realizing it was only a short time before the islands would become a bitter sweet memory, I awoke to the realization that there was more to the islands then previously thought. During the sixteen months of being confronted with daily environmental challenges I was oblivious to their natural splendor. It seemed almost sinful to have overlooked their awesome beauty. It's now after the fact, but I couldn't help recalling the daily ground tremors we experienced. Fantasy or not, I concluded it was nature nudging me to look beyond the hostile living experiences and appreciate, what someday, will be a treasure of beautiful memories.

The island's towering palm trees were hallmarks of regal beauty, easily observed but also easily overlooked. The surrounding seas teemed with endless schools of luminous fish darting through crystal clear waters. The muted tones of dense jungle greenery was habitat to countless birds whose brilliant plumage shamed the rainbows that frequently arched overhead. It was on the eve of my departure that I appreciated the flip side of the islands that had challenged my teenage years for sixteen months. And it was then, I also realized, how fortunate I was to spend these years in such an exotic setting. As the islands gradually faded below the horizon I experienced a bittersweet feeling, wondering if I would ever see them again, it was August 24, 1944.

Nepoui

On September 1, 1944, we anchored in Nepoui Harbor, New Caledonia, peaceful, welcoming setting approximately a hundred miles from Noumea, our first port of call. Our camp was located on top of a high bluff overlooking the harbor and a country setting of small, family owned coffee plantations. It was a welcomed pleasure returning to a moderate climate and friendly environment where the nights were cool enough to require a blanket. The purpose of this mission was two fold: supply the battalion with new equipment and rehabilitate the personnel in preparation for the next assignment. Interspersed with the rehabilitation program, the battalion constructed a pier to provide a deep water facility for cargo vessels to unload at dockside rather than barge the cargo to shore. Though this mega pier was completed on schedule, it was never used for it's intended purpose as the war zone progressed more rapidly than anticipated.

Rest and rehabilitation was just that, a relief from the daily work routines we experienced since leaving the states. Between minor work details, there was ample opportunity to explore the island and engage in activities other than Navy assigned duties. Taking full advantage of this rare opportunity, a tent mate, J. C. Murphy, and I combined our limited skills to build a sailboat. It was fourteen feet long, constructed of scrap wood and equipped with a sail fashioned from a bed sheet. Considering there were no plans, and just sheer guess work, all went well except for locating the mast. During the maiden voyage, with a brisk wind filling the sail, the bow began plowing under water that nearly submerged us. After realizing we located the mast to far forward, the mistake was corrected allowing us several months of pleasant sailing.

The harbor where we sailed abounded with fish and the countryside was just as abundant with deer, both of which presented the opportunity to change a very predictable menu. To provide for this, conventional sportsman like conduct went out the window. To go fishing simply meant dropping a hand grenade in the water and wait for the stunned fish to surface. The rapid-fire capability of carbine rifles was no less a match for the deer than the grenades were for the fish. It was unorthodox, un-sportsman-like and irresponsible, but very effective in providing the battalion with fresh meat and fish.

One of my most treasured memories of New Caledonia, and perhaps the South Pacific, were our lunch visits to an elderly French gentleman. He lived in a densely wooded area in a house with a thatched roof extending over an open porch that was a haven for a countless number of colorful birds. Under the thatched porch hung many pots of vibrant colored tropical flowers. The house was situated on a gentle bluff close to a swift following stream that formed a natural swimming hole we used while lunch was being prepared, the setting was a post card picture of a country house. The lunch included platters of fried eggs, steak, salad, French bread and wine, the meal was complemented with a salad from his own fruit trees. The charge for this exceptionally delicious meal was a barter arrangement rather than a cash fee. Our host was always in need of gasoline to keep his vintage car and farm equipment running. Since we had access to this, though not legitimately, his need was provided in exchange for many memorable days of swimming and feasting. At the time of our last good-bye, shortly before departing, New Caledonia, he requested I send him vegetable seeds upon my return home. Many months later I was able to fulfill his wish, and it was my final contact with this gracious gentleman.

Eniwetok and Ulithi

News about our pending departure was received with mixed emotions as it meant, trading a comfortable, home-like camp for an uncertain future. However, our concern was cushioned by the pleasant thought that every move we made was one more closer to the home we left two years before. My daily Mass intention was offered for our safe return, and that it would become a reality in the not too distant future. Hopefully this move was a silent answer to my prayer. It was May 2, 1945, when the USS Celeno set sail from the idle dock in Nepoui harbor, for another unknown, "Island X". Soon after we left port the commander announced our destination was Eniwetok in the Central Pacific. On day five of the voyage, the Commander assembled all hands on deck to announce that Germany surrendered and the war in Europe was over. Following a brief service of thanksgiving the battalion band entertained while we rejoiced about this historic and much prayed for news. It was May 7, 1945. There was widespread speculation that Japan would soon follow.

Four days later, May 11, 1945, we arrived at Eniwetok, an uninhabited coral atoll in the Central Pacific that was barely above sea level. As the ship entered the atoll, the clarity of the water was so crystal clear, it appeared as if it was going aground. Within this protective anchorage there were dozens of ships which indicated that Eniwetok was a staging area for a future operation. We remained aboard ship except for periods of recreational time on the beach. Shipboard time evolved into a boring rumor mill that further evolved into additional rumors, always speculating, where and when we go from here.

On May 20, 1945, there was no further need for any more guessing games as we sailed from Eniwetok to Ulithi, another uninhabited atoll that was a carbon copy of our previous anchorage. It was, May 25, 1945. Time was taxing our patience since it had been seven weeks since we left New Caledonia and we remained clueless as to our destination and it's purpose. To alleviate shipboard restlessness, shore parties were planned to relieve this stress which was a welcome relief and an opportunity to play softball, enjoy a few beers and stretch our sea legs on solid ground.

Bloody Battle of Okinawa

Okinawa was the bloodiest battle of World War II's Pacific campaign. More people died at Okinawa than all those killed during the atomic bombings of Hiroshima and Nagasaki. Casualties totaled more than 38,000 Americans wounded and 12,000 killed or missing, more than 107,000 Japanese and Okinawan conscripts killed, and perhaps 100,000 Okinawan civilians who perished in the battle.

American losses at Okinawa were so heavy as to elicit congressional calls for an investigation into the conduct of the military commanders. The cost of this battle, in terms of lives, time, and material, weighed heavily in the decision to use the atomic bomb against Japan just six weeks later.

The battle for Okinawa began on a relatively calm note when the 1st and 6th Marine Divisions and 7th and 96th Army Divisions landed April 1, 1945 on the southwest coast. But then the American forces ran into the Shuri defense line that General Mitsuri Ushijima, commander of the Japanese forces on Okinawa, had constructed. There ensued three weeks of bitter, cave-to-cave fighting before the defense line was breached.

On June 21, 83 days of fighting came to an end when Ushijima came out at dawn from his cave bunker and before his subordinates committed hara-kiri.

SOURCES: GlobalSecurity.org, Chronicle of the 20th Century

Okinawa

On the morning of, June 12, 1945, it was anchors aweigh as we sailed from the safe refuge of Ulithi for another unnamed destination. However, it wasn't long after we were jolted out of our lethargy when it was announced we were enroute to Okinawa. Okinawa was the threshold to the Japanese Empire. The next logical move would be the Japanese mainland. It took six days to reach Okinawa, and each one was filled with anxiety, and unrelenting rumors to what could be expected. The ships daily news bulletins vividly detailed the intensity of the Okinawa engagement further elevating the adrenaline surge being experienced This was, Japan's last line of defense, after which, further action would be on their own soil.

On June 18, 1945, the ship anchored a comfortable distance from the principal harbor of Naha, the capitol city. From aboard ship, we witnessed the onshore battle. During the day it was noise and smoke. At night the sky was brightly illuminated with tracer bullets and flares from exploding bombs and shells. The battle was for Shuri Castle, the Japanese stronghold. It was a do or die engagement for them. Losing it meant the loss of Okinawa. We remained aboard ship approximately a week witnessing this historic engagement and then went ashore following the surrender. The primary purpose of this mission was to build a landing strip for B- 29 bombers and hangars to service them as well as restoring the island's infrastructure badly damaged from the recent battle. The Okinawa people were cautiously friendly, but somewhat suspicious of our presence. They conscientiously worked their small farms and rice paddies that were fertilized with human waste. They lived in small thatched roof houses surrounded by expansive growths of trees. Each family had their own burial tomb that was oval in shape to represent a pregnant woman's stomach. Beneath this rounded dome was an opening, through which the deceased is interned in a large earthen vase. In accordance with their belief in reincarnation, the urn contained rice, coins and small artifacts deemed necessary for the return trip. Many of the tombs were used for bomb shelters by the Japanese and pilfered by the military for souvenirs and other valuables.

On August 6, 1945 a B-29 bomber, named Enola Gay, dropped a bomb on Hiroshima that completely obliterated the city. Three days later, Nagasaki, was also devastated by a similar bomb. A strange word suddenly became part of our vocabulary, "atomic," a definition that was incomprehensible. And it was beyond our intellect to comprehend how a single device could annihilate an entire city. Five days later, Japan surrendered, it was August 15, 1945, V. J. Day. The day we so anxiously awaited finally arrived and with it our thoughts turned to home.

I was originally scheduled to sail home on, September 30, 1945, however, a devastating typhoon struck Okinawa just prior to this date that caused catastrophic damage to many of the military installations. All home bound schedules for Sea Bee personnel were cancelled until after the damaged facilities were repaired. It was after the storm when it was realized the natives encircled their houses with trees to provide a wind barrier against typhoons. Except for some missing thatch, they survived unscathed.

Homeward bound

The long, anxiously awaited trip home began on October 25, 1945, when we sailed from, Naha harbor aboard an amphibious attack ship destined for Seattle, Washington. This was to become my most harrowing experience, equal to none, that I endured during the previous twenty-eight months. While enroute, via the great north pacific route, weather conditions turned horrifying. Gale force winds created mountainous waves that crested high as the navigation bridge. The pouring rain turned to hail, then snow, aggravating our discomfort, being dressed in tropical clothes. The most terrifying concern was my fear the ship would roll over and I would become a casualty of a war that had already ended. At times I truly felt it was a strong possibility. The ocean eventually calmed, and with it, weather improved and my seasickness was a sour memory.

After sixteen apprehensive days, I kept wondering if we would ever arrive home safely. With this thought fresh in my mind, a coastline appeared faintly through early morning fog. If what was thought to be a coast line, was indeed the United States, it was an answer to a multitude of prayers. Shortly after, an announcement confirmed it was the Washington coast. The ship sailed into Puget Sound, docking at the Navy base in Port Angles, Seattle. It was November 10, 1945, twenty eight months to the day since we left Port Hueneme for the South Pacific, on July 10, 1943. At the time, Port Angles was a major navy base and a processing hub for personnel returning from the Pacific. It was also an orientation center for personnel being assigned to state side duty prior to discharge.

During our brief stay, we received a cursory physical exam, a sea bag with a set of new uniforms and orders for our next assignment. It also provided an opportunity to finalize travel plans for the trip home. My plan was to be home for Thanksgiving Day, and because of this I had to settle for whatever seating was available. My only choice was a train between Seattle and Chicago, that turned out to be a vintage coach with minimal amenities, and stone hard, rattan seats. Upon arriving in Chicago, after sitting up for almost forty eight hours, I secured a reserved seat on the Chicago Limited, a premier train to New York City. After sitting on a granite like seat for two days, the luxury of an upholstered recliner lulled me into a deep sleep, awakening shortly before arriving in Grand Central Station. I showered and changed uniform in the USO facilities at Grand Central before taking the subway and bus to Throgs Neck, and the home I had left thirty-two months ago.

When I arrived at the last stop of my 27,000-mile journey, I hesitated to leave the security of the bus and walk the short distance home in what I envisioned a strange neighborhood. I was also overly anxious anticipating the family's reaction to my unannounced arrival. When our next door neighbor, Mrs. Nester, waved to me from her apartment window to warmly welcome me home, her kind greeting reassured me that I returned to the same friendly neighborhood that I left. With my emotions running high, the familiar sound of the creaking wooden stairs was music to my ears. Without knocking, I opened the door and saw my sister, Doris, sitting on the sofa. Her surprised response was enough for Mom to hurry from the kitchen, dressed in her usual, full-length apron, greeting me with a long, tearful, heart-warming embrace. Her first controlled words, clasping her warm hands to my face were, "Oh my, you're shaving!" It was all so sudden, unexpected and exciting. Misty eyed, we both stumbled for something intelligent to say. It was truly an answer to all my prayers and mass intentions to be safely back in the comfort of my own home, a luxury that was previously taken for granted.

Dad was still working out of state so we didn't meet until several days later when he returned home for Thanksgiving. Our greeting, though warm and friendly, hardly measured up to the one with Mom. Thanksgiving dinner was typical of the many I so thoroughly enjoyed in the past and so vividly thought about in the South Pacific.

Eventually, I began to renew acquaintances with neighborhood friends who also returned from active duty. Four did not: Eddie Schields, Herman Walker, Charlie Fetzer and Alex Rosenbloom - four young men from Logan Avenue who made the ultimate sacrifice. In addition to these friends, my cousin, Bob (Buster) Croke, lost his life aboard the U.S.S. Beatty when it was bombed and sank off the coast of Italy on, November 9, 1944.

I was honorably discharged on, January 18, 1946, as a Carpenter's mate, 2nd class. I was awarded the Asiatic Pacific Ribbon, with four stars, and the American Theatre and Victory Ribbons. I re-enlisted in the United States Naval Reserve on October 1, 1946, and honorably discharged as a Yeoman 1st class on September 30,1954.

Very active at 90, Bob Clancy is still volunteering with several community groups, as he has for thirty years. He has five grand children and three great grandchildren. While he is proud of his USMC grandson, a career Marine, who has had six-month deployments to Iraq and Afghanistan, he still remembers his thirty consecutive months away from home. He also notes the contrast between today's up to the minute news, broadcast to friend and foe alike, and his confinement to base for weeks prior to embarkation, lest "military secrets" be disclosed.

Bob Clancy, back row, third from left

Eight Delaware boys in the 82nd

82nd U. S. Naval Construction Battalion
FPO., San Francisco, Calif.

LIBERTY PASS

The bearer Clancy, R. N., CM3c
is attached to this organization and
does not possess the proper liberty
uniform due to his recent return from
the forward area.

He is on authorized liberty, beginning

0800 - 15 January   1945 and

expiring 0700 - 20 Jan.   1945

Officer-in-Charge   Paul E. Seufer
                                 Exec. Officer

CATHOLIC MASS

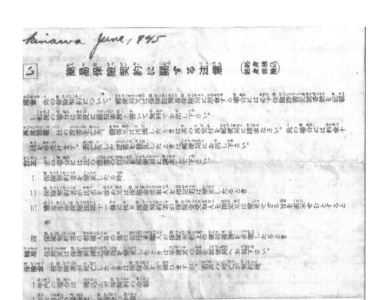

Message from Okinawa

Cuban crab migration leaves a huge mess — and an opportunity

The Sterling Island phenomena is confirmed!

Left Port Hueneme, California — July 10, 1943
Crossed The Equator — " 18, "
arrived at New Caledonia — " 28, "
Left New Caledonia — August 15, "
arrived at Guadalcanal — " 19 ..
Left Guadalcanal — September 19 :
arrived at Munda — " 20 ..
Left Munda — " 21 "
arrived at Onpongpa — " 21 "
Left Ondonga — Dec 1st "
arrived at Munda — " 1st "
Left Munda — Dec 14 "
arrived at Sterling Island — " 15 "
Left Sterling Island — aug 24, 1944
arrived at New Caledonia, Nepoui — Sept 1st "
Left New Caledonia, Nepoui — May 2nd 1945
arrived Eniwetok, Marshall Is. — May 4th "
Left Eniwetok Marshall Is. — May 20th "
arrived Ulithi Caroline Is. — May 25th "
Left Ulithi Caroline Is. — June 12th "
arrived, Okinawa, Ryukyus. — June 18th "
Left Okinawa, Ryukyus — Oct 25th "
arrived Seattle, U.S.A — Nov 10th "

Clancys Log of 27,080 miles
July 1943 – Nov 1945

73

February 12, 1946

My dear Mr. Clancy:

I have addressed this letter to reach you after
all the formalities of your separation from active service
are completed. I have done so because, without formality but
as clearly as I know how to say it, I want the Navy's pride in
you, which it is my privilege to express, to reach into your
civil life and to remain with you always.

You have served in the greatest Navy in the world.

It crushed two enemy fleets at once, receiving their
surrenders only four months apart.

It brought our land-based airpower within bombing
range of the enemy, and set our ground armies on the beachheads
of final victory.

It performed the multitude of tasks necessary to
support these military operations.

No other Navy at any time has done so much. For
your part in these achievements you deserve to be proud as
long as you live. The Nation which you served at a time of
crisis will remember you with gratitude.

The best wishes of the Navy go with you into civilian
life. Good luck!

Sincerely yours,

James Forrestal

James Forrestal

Mr. Robert Nicholas Clancy
271 Logan Ave.
New York 61, New York

From One Marine to Another
by Elinor Stratton
(A seventeen year old war bride)
As told to John Reardon   Oct 2015

Today, we can hardly imagine just how tough things were during the Great Depression, the formative years of the Greatest Generation. But, imagine if you will, a time before welfare and food stamps. A time of breadlines and starvation. And a time when mothers and children were often left alone to cope, as husbands searched for work. And imagine what would become of such a child, if perhaps his mother became ill, and died, when he was only twelve.

In just a few short years, just approaching age sixteen, Bill Stratton had dropped out of school, and was living in a one room shack with his coal miner father. He was feeding and caring for the mules, a "mule boy."

The CCC seemed like a better option, but when he and a friend tried to apply, they found they were ineligible, since their families weren't "on relief." Heading home, they saw the Marine recruiting office and stopped in. They were invited to come back the next day to go to Altoona, Pa. to take a physical. Bill showed up; his friend didn't. With the war looming, the military was building up, and apparently age was a minor issue. And so it was, in April, 1941, that young William Paul Stratton was off to Parris Island, and the United States Marine Corps.

The training at Parris Island really "weeded out" many young recruits. But Bill was determined to make it. The "DI" stood by his bunk two nights, thinking it was Bill crying. However, the "DI" listened carefully and decided it was not Bill. The recruit in the next bunk was called out of line the next morning and was never seen again.

After basic training, while at Quantico, Bill's true age was revealed by an aunt and uncle. Upon questioning, Bill told the officer that he "had found a home," and was happy to be a Marine. The officer told the relatives that since they hadn't cared enough when Bill needed a home, they could leave the base and stop causing trouble. He then told Bill that they would "put some miles" between him and the relatives. So he was sent to the West Coast and then to Hawaii.

And so it was on December 7, 1941, that a sixteen year old Marine, stationed at Pearl Harbor became a "Pearl Harbor Survivor." He was later officially listed as the fourth youngest!

During the attack on Pearl Harbor, Bill found himself down at the docks. He was knocked down, and briefly rendered unconscious when the USS Shaw was hit by bombs. When he came to, he and many others started to pull sailors out of the water as they struggled ashore. (How greatly this affected him was seen years later, when he refused to view the movie "Titanic." He simply said, "If you had tried to save people who were crying out for help, you would understand.")

In a very short time after Pearl Harbor, Stratton was part of a very small contingent of Marines sent to a very small spec of an island in the Pacific. Palmyra Atoll was, like Wake Island, one of the last western most islands between Hawaii and the Japanese threat that was fast engulfing the Pacific.

After a defensive year in the Pacific, before our island hopping offense took hold, the 17 year old "veteran" was given a short leave in February 1943. He promptly proposed to his 17 year old girlfriend, before reporting to Camp LeJeune, N.C., to "instruct" the "young boys."

In June he managed another ten day leave during which he saw his girlfriend graduate from high school and then married her. On July 19, 1943, the young bride saw him for the last time until the war would be over. Among other trials, there were two month-long intervals in 1944, and 1945, when she received "no mail" from him. This was during the time that the papers were reporting some of the heaviest fighting in the Pacific.

And he was "somewhere in the Pacific." He took part in regaining the Marshall Islands, and was in the **first wave at Iwo Jima,** where, after twenty nine days on the island, he was one of only twelve members of his company to survive uninjured.

He always remembered one night in particular on Iwo Jima. Separated form his friends, frightened, and completely alone, he "called out to God, to see him through." After he made a solemn vow to always help others in need, he had "a most complete feeling of peace," and knew he would be ok. (In later life, he would often "be there," just when someone was in need.)

(Other "later life" instances included:
A "discussion" with a minister in which Bill persuaded the minister to realize that "millions of lives on both sides were saved by the A Bombs." Most veterans agreed that after the fanatical way the Japanese had fought on Iwo Jima, and for eighty two days on Okinawa, it was clear that the Japanese would never have surrendered otherwise.

An "interview" with a Japanese newsman at the Iwo Jima Monument in Washington DC. Bill was too overcome with emotion to continue.

Television coverage from an Iwo Jima reunion of former enemies. When Bill saw them hugging each other, he tearfully and simply said, "I don't think I ever could have done that."

After Iwo Jima, Bill's next stop was back to Guam, where earlier he had helped "mop up." This time, he happened to meet several Marines from his home town, including one he had known as a young boy growing up.

There was also the instance (possibly in Hawaii) when he had to earn the respect of an older Marine who resented taking orders from an eighteen year old corporal. After several weeks of dirty details, they came to an understanding and eventually became friends. They even visited after the war!

These and many other young men were preparing for the massive invasion of mainland Japan, and expecting heavy casualties.

Instead, the war ended abruptly when the bomb was dropped. From Guam, with well over a hundred "rotation points," Bill fully expected to be going home. His orders however sent him to Sasebo, Japan, a large Japanese Naval Base, for "occupation." His protests to the commanding officer were met with a promise, "from one Marine to another." If he would stay just ten days, "touring the land of your former enemy," he would be on a homeward bound ship on the eleventh day.

The promise was kept. Apparently, it meant a lot to that officer to see a Pearl Harbor and Iwo Jima survivor come full circle

Semper Fi

Saipan Scoop

Fourth Division USMC

Saipan Scoop

Bob Austin
As told to John Reardon
Nov 2015

In June of 1944, many a mother prayed, knowing her son was involved in a D-day amphibious landing. Bob Austin knew that his now widowed mother was praying for all three of her sons. By June 15, he had landed on Saipan and his two brothers were already ashore in Europe.

When the war was over, and the brothers compared notes, Bob was once again reminded that there "really were two wars." True, both his brothers went ashore in Europe and stayed "for the duration." And it was no picnic. But what is this they are saying about USO shows, the girls in Paris, and advancing a hundred miles a day? Bob's advances were always measured in yards. And forget about girls and the USO. They were unknown.

The first objective at Saipan was "only" 1000 yards inland, but "we never got off the beach." Bob's unit arrived at H+6. Many ahead of him did not survive. During the invasion, Bob was captain of a five man fifty caliber machine gun crew, providing security for Batteries D, E, and F, of the second battalion, fourteenth artillery. He remembers the next days were 24/7 under fire.

Later, the Marines advanced on both left and right. But in one of the war's great controversies, as Bob says, "the army, in the middle, had a different approach." They did not advance as quickly, and the Marines' flanks were exposed. (The Army General was relieved of his command, and Marine General "Howlin Mad" Smith replaced him.) Vicious fighting ensued for days before Saipan fell.

Bob can only speak for Saipan and Tinian (where he was again captain of the gun crew.) He participated in both amphibious assaults. Both were major battles for the Marines, and both became ever more significant as the war progressed: Saipan was the first position from which land based US bombers were able to reach the Japanese mainland. And Tinian became the base from which the A bombs were launched.

At Tinian, Bob gives a lot of credit to the Seabees. The invasion was a masterstroke of deception. Only the southern beaches were vulnerable. The northern beach was rocky, narrow and mountainous. It would have been "impossible" to land there. So, after a feint toward the south, where all the defenses were, and the reinforcements were being sent, the assault was made in the north – Seabees first. In their "combat bulldozers," they quickly cleared the way, and the Marines were able to establish a strong perimeter by nightfall.

He remembers how strongly the enemy "pillboxes" were built. Twelve inches of concrete, covered with strong palm logs and sand. Our shelling "only rearranged the sand." He remembers that they could only be taken by flamethrowers. And he remembers the screams and the smell of burning flesh. Bob says that the movies can come close with the sights and sounds, but they cannot capture the smells of a battlefield. In later years, even an accidental charring at a barbecue could be reminiscent.

After the initial landings, Bob's duty would revert to artillery, and he was usually 400 yards from the front. But they were always targets, and often came under banzai attacks. He counts at least six times he "should have been killed." The first was when two enemy mortar shells landed directly between him and a friend. Both shells were duds!

On another occasion, when their vehicle stalled, they were spotted by an enemy sniper. "Have you ever seen six men take cover behind one jeep tire?" Minutes after they were able to withdraw, they saw their former position "obliterated" by enemy mortar.

He also remembers manning an outpost one night. There were no radios – just a long wire to be pulled in case of trouble. The other end of the wire would rattle some stones in tin cans to alert the officer. When a Jap snuck in behind the outpost, he had the misfortune to fumble with his grenade just long enough to be too slow. He was quickly seen and neutralized. Their tugs on the wire went unanswered 'til morning, when the Lieutenant arrived and proceeded to ream them for making so much noise during the night. His expression and demeanor changed dramatically when he was finally asked what should be done with the dead Jap's body.

Another sad memory of Tinian also persists. The civilian population had been persuaded by the enemy that suicide would be preferable to being captured by the Marines. Many were seen leaping from the cliffs to their deaths. The water below ran red with their blood. Bob is reluctant to tell all he remembers, but feels strongly that each generation should study history, rather than have to repeat it. He also feels strongly that there is no doubt that the A bomb had to be used, and that it actually saved many lives, American and Japanese.

There is yet another "bull story" that Bob couldn't resist telling. It had to do with the cisterns. There was no fresh water on Tinian, except rainwater, channeled to large cisterns. He and a buddy had occasion to be walking toward the cistern for water, when they became aware of a cow behind them. Livestock roamed freely. And behind the cow was a bull. In a very short time, the buddy had mounted the wall, and the bull had started to charge Bob. Instinct took over, and he literally "grabbed the bull by the horns," and flipped him. It gave just enough time to leap atop the the wall. He soon had a new nickname, "Tex."

In this skirmish, Bob shed blood (from his big toe) and a welt was raised across his chest, but no purple heart was awarded. It could not be confirmed that the bull was Japanese.

Some of Bob's other random memories of Saipan were recorded on a Jap notebook that he eventually "liberated:" (Taking notes was a serious offense.)

The coral was so hard that you couldn't dig a two inch foxhole. And a bulldozer would only go two more inches.

You were lucky to get one quart of water per day, and that was from large oil cans. To kill the taste, you shaved c-rations into it.

Our basic food was C and K rations which we carried ashore in our knapsacks. Eventually, we were issued "Ones," to feed ten men for a day, or one man for ten days.

Our first hot meal served by cooks was after the island was declared "secure."

"Pop" was lucky to get that fumbling Jap first. His safety was on, and he too was fumbling and cussing.

As a personnel classification expert, Bob's skills in that area were not needed 'til after the battle. So, he became head of a gun crew of cooks, mechanics and other clerks. Every marine is a rifleman first. Your job was "whatever it takes – 24/7."

There were 2,000 casualties on the first day, and 10,000 by day 15. That was 50% of the 4th division.

Many of the troops suffered from malaria, dengue fever, (bonecrusher), or excessive diarrhea.

"Saipan Scoop" was the name of the on-board newsletter while enroute from Hawaii to Saipan. (Several copies survive.)

"Mail call" was held whenever possible. It could be a morale builder or a depressant, depending on whether or not one received mail. Most days, nothing. One day, I received eight letters, three from my mother, and five from my girlfriend (now my wife of seventy years.)

But back to the beginning. Dec. 7, 1941, "the day of infamy," was also the day from which Bob Austin marked his own wartime service. It was his first day on a new job. He had just been hired by the civil service to work with the US Navy in Washington, D.C. He progressed rapidly, often being in the "right place at the right time," and was soon offered a CPO rating "for the duration," if he'd agree to stay there on the job.

But instead, after a year of war, Bob volunteered for the Marines, "for the duration, plus six months," and in December of 1942, he started his three years of wartime service. This was when he missed his own going away party. It was arranged for a week before his scheduled departure, but on that afternoon, he learned his departure had been advanced by seven days. He heard it was a nice party.

His year in the Pacific, marked by the landings at Saipan and Tinian, was bracketed by two "lucky" stateside tours. After basic training, 95% of the troops were sent to the fleet in the Pacific. Bob, possibly because of his prior duty(?), was assigned for additional training and some stateside duty as a personnel classification specialist before leaving for Maui in late 1943.

Several interesting memories date to this period of his service. He had made some extra money working as a lifeguard that summer, to buy an engagement ring. In the Fall, he requested that his pre-deployment furlough be scheduled a little early. (So he could propose before leaving.) He returned to Camp LeJeune in three days, and in three more days, all leaves were cancelled and they shipped to the west coast.

When Bob arrived in California, he was "ten weeks ahead of his pay records." He survived by working part time at a nearby aircraft assembly plant. Many servicemen would work whenever they could, being paid in cash at the end of each shift.

Bob also "felt the hand of God" as another leave was ending. Following his leave for his father's death, as he was boarding a bus to return to the west coast, the chimes at St. Stephen's church in Wilkes-barre, Pa, were playing "God be with you 'til we meet again." HE was!

From California, they shipped for Maui in late 1943, and then spent most of 1944 in amphibious training, landings and combat. Having survived, and having earned rotation points, Bob next remembers arriving in San Francisco, with only the clothes on his back. Combat clothes. Technically, "out of uniform" for a liberty in town. It was a wise officer who issued special passes reading "Returning from combat, authorized to be out of uniform."

He was soon "lucky" enough to be indentified as officer material, and in late 1944 was sent to college at Villanova, in Philadelphia, in preparation for OTS. So he has fond memories of being stateside at war's end.

But, he says, it was an entirely different world back then. For example, he remembers at the time of his discharge, he didn't even have the eight cents needed for bus fare from the base. His first post war job paid twenty dollars a week.

Overall, Bob Austin, at a healthy 93, considers himself blessed to have survived. He is convinced that the Lord had a reason for his long life, and he has tried to help others throughout a long life of volunteer service.

His wife, of seventy years, calls him a "relic" of history. But that's ok with him, as he happily participates in various living history events, talks and parades. He can still wear his original Marine uniform, complete with his awards: Pacific Theater with two battle stars, American Theater, Presidential Unit Citation, Good Conduct, and WW II Victory medal.

And he's still looking for another couple that has been married seventy years.

Perhaps Bob Austin's experiences are best captured and shared in a poem that he wrote back in 1979. He reads it dramatically, with the emotion and cadence that could only come from one who has lived it. He graciously shares it here:

BEACH BLUE TWO
by Bob Austin
1979

BRIEFING

Fourteen June, nineteen forty four,
  Marianna Islands: Saipan.
On the island there are only two cities:
  Charan-Kanoa and Garapan.
The rest is all cane plantations,
  small farms and countryside.
It's only a mere twelve miles long
  and five and a half miles wide.

Mount Topatchau's in the center,
  Mount Fina Susu to the south.
There may be Chomoro villages
  at Lake Susupe's mouth.
It's only twelve hundred miles from Tokyo,
  about four hours by air.
We're assaulting Saipan in the morning,
  so let the Japanese beware!

There's a village called Aslito,
  an airstrip by its side.
That's our prime objective,
  one we must not be denied.
Just everybody fight like hell,
  and we'll all see the day

When we'll have traversed the atoll
east to Magicienne Bay.

There'll be reinforced Marine Divisions,
The Second and the Fourth.
Fourth will land on Beach Blue Two,
The second on Red to the North.
Twenty days from tomorrow,
victory should be within our reach.
Good luck, and may God keep you -
Tomorrow morning we hit the beach.

D-DAY

Fifteen June, reveille at 0 three hundred-
chow at three fifteen.
It's the best marine corps breakfast
the men have ever seen.
All the steak that one could eat
with ice cream for dessert.
Troops gorge upon that sumptuous food
until their bellies hurt.

Debarkation at 0 six hundred,
down nets into waiting craft
Go fighting men by the hundreds,
'midships, fore and aft.
Beyond the range of land-based guns
the landing craft rendezvous,
Gathering together at the departure line
for the assault on Beach Blue Two.

"Now, all synchronize your watches!"
"Have you got your bayonet?"
"Check your gas masks, socks and rations,"
"Don't get your rifles wet."

"All heads down 'cept the cox'n's
   he's the one who's got to see."
"By this time tomorrow morning
   I wonder where we'll be?"

Huge battle-wagon cannon
   that have been firing since four,
Belch fire, death and destruction
   upon the tropic shore.
They suddenly fall silent,
   leaving a quiet that hurts the ear.
The "softening up" is over,
   invasion time draws near.

The landing craft leap forward,
   speeding o'er the ocean swell.
The valiant men inside those boats
   are being carried into hell.
Toward the distant shore they go
   in evasive zig zag lines,
Evading deadly shell bursts
   and floating undersea mines.

When the assault craft are still
   a long way from shore,
Large caliber Jap guns
   open up with a deafening roar,
The shelling takes a heart-rending toll
   Of the unwieldy craft nearing the tiny atol.

Many LCVPs and LCIs are damaged, wrecked or sunk,
Hundreds of men upon the decks find rest in a watery bunk.
Thousands more will meet their death
   before this day is through.
But the assault waves have landed
   on the sands of Beach Blue Two.

THE BEACH

The chatter of machine guns
    joins the small arms fire.
The deafening sounds crescendo
    as the battle pitch rises higher.
The coral isle is honeycombed
    with pillboxes, tunnels and caves,
From Topatchau's commanding height
    to the coastline's screaming waves.

Wreckage of boats and equipment
    increases hour by hour,
Attesting to our enemy's
    awesome defensive power.
From the cavernous maws of LST's
    pour supplies and ammunition,
Vitally needed by embattled Marines
    to strengthen their position.

Eviscerated corpses
    lie strewn upon the strand.
The blood of the dead and dying
    reddens sea and land,
The smell of burning and rotting flesh
    permeates the air.
And the pitiful cry of "Corpsman"
    is heard 'most everywhere.

A lone Jap Zero appears on the scene,
    streaming out of the sun,
Swiftly traversing the crowded beach
    in a murderous strafing run.
A flame-thrower team attacks a cave,
    releasing a lethal stream.
The immolated defenders scream –
    and scream - and scream.

Jap firepower shows in strength,
  pinning troops upon the beach.
They can see their day's objective
  but it is not within their reach.
"Up and over the seawall,
  you can't stay here all day,
Move out you fighting Leathernecks,
  there'll be no rest today."

The casualty toll mounts higher,
  in this bloodiest battle to date.
Heroism is commonplace
  as men go forth to meet their fate,
With bulldog-like tenacity
  the landing party has endured.
After repulsing a final counter-attack
  Beach Blue is now "secured."

EPILOGUE
In a span of several hours
  men have aged by many years,
Have come to grips with war and death,
  with tragedies and fears.
They are homesick, hungry, frightened,
  weary and distraught,
They will ever carry the mental scars
  of the battle they have fought.
The heroes of this battle
  came thousands of miles to die
Upon this tiny atoll
  beneath the blue Pacific sky,
The survivors humbly thank their God
  that they've lived safely through.
The carnage and devastation
  that was bloody Beach Blue Two.

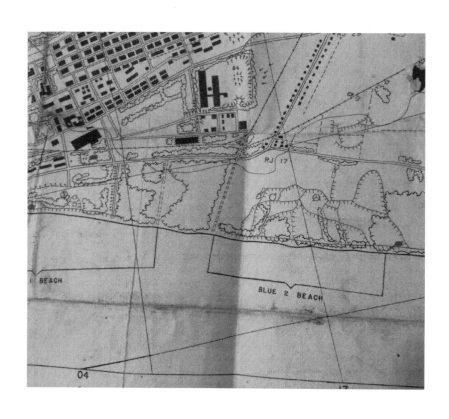

Beach Blue Two
Saipan, 1944

A Day in the Life of a Crewmember

Clifford E. Chronister

3241d Bomb Squadron, 30lst Bomb Group,
15th Air Force
Contributed by Connie Reichardt

About 4 PM the day before a bomb run an orderly would post the list of flyers, all crew members, plane numbers and the position of your plane in the group formation. These plane numbers were subject to change depending on the number of returning planes and their damage assessments. The ground crews and chiefs had to work all night repairing and preparing their planes for the following day plus refueling and loading the bombs. Each squadron had to put up 7 to 9 planes every day and usually there would be 6 or 8 groups making up a mission.

After seeing your name on the battle order for the next day, you had to prepare yourself and get your equipment together. I carried my 45 caliber side arm and a few 45 caliber buck shot cartridges which were to help with survival if you were shot down in enemy territory.

Most of the equipment was kept in a flight bag in a building about two miles away from our tents but near the runway. In the bag were my parachute and harness, Mae West, electric heated suit, oxygen mask, leather helmet and headset, flak jacket, steel helmet, electric gloves and shoes.

We lived in a walled tent with a brick floor, in an olive grove near Foggia, in southern Italy. There were five or six enlisted men to each tent and we slept on cots. The number of men would vary as planes were shot down and then a bunk would be empty for a while.

On mission days, about 3 AM, an orderly would come through camp blowing a whistle to wake all men who were on the battle order for that day. As you crawled out of bed, you wondered if you would be sleeping here tomorrow night.

As you prepared yourself for the day, you had personal things to do; go to the mess hall for breakfast, shave etc. Full beards were not allowed because the oxygen mask would leak. No pull on boots or shoes were allowed. If you bailed out your boots might fly off. As Aerial Gunner Engineer, I was assigned to bring food and drink to the plane for the return flight. At the mess hall, I was given four small thermoses of coffee and ten spam sandwiches that were packed to take to the plane.

A six by six truck would come and take the enlisted men to the briefing room which was about two miles away. All crew members would meet there. When the curtain was pulled back it revealed the target of the day, also a first and second alternate target. At this time all would be told how many fighters to expect and the number of anti aircraft guns that were placed around the target. Now the enlisted men were dismissed and another two miles back to the equipment shack to pick up their flight gear that they had stowed after their last mission. Then on to the plane you were assigned for that day.

It was still dark but we would have to get all our gear and equipment in place. Also, check the guns and thread the ammo belts into each gun. There were 13 guns on a B 17, five were double mounts, and there were three single mounts. We would wait for the officers to arrive and then wait for the sun to come up.

As it gets brighter we watch the tower for the first flare, signaling to start engines, the next flair would signal for the leader to start his roll for the take off. As soon as his wheels left the ground the next plane would start his roll.

With each pilot trying to keep up and maintain his position in the formation, we would now be burning 450 gallons of fuel per hour. Total fuel was 2,800 gallons. Our bomb load was 6,000 pounds. The radios were quiet except for reporting in to the pilot.

Before we reached 10,000 feet I would go into the bomb bay area and remove the pins from each of the bomb fuses both front and back. Now the bombs were armed and I would return to my upper turret and go on oxygen.

Not much to do now except pray. We had been cruising at 150 mph and were now about 600 miles from our home base at an altitude of approximately 24-28,000 feet.

We are now at the I.P. (Initial Point.) This is the most dangerous part of a mission, called the '"bomb run," from the I.P. to the target. Bombs away around 10 to 15 minutes. During this time the plane is turned over to the bombardier to guide it over the target. Because of all the anti aircraft shells exploding, the fighters don't usually attack at this time.

Now, with bombs dropped, the group heads for home. Each pilot must check for plane damage and each gunner must keep alert for fighter attack. We were still very vulnerable and if a plane was shot down all gunners were required to follow it down by sight, and count the parachutes that got out. At this time the pilot called to each crew member to check in and report if wounded or not.

During our return, while we are still 400 miles in enemy territory, we know that one burst of flack could still bring down a plane. An hour or two later we clear the coast and fly over the Adriatic Ocean. No flack over the water.

As we near our home field we hear the pilot call the tower (Long Shirt) with our coded name. Now we can relax with the thought that we will live another day.

From August to December, 1944, our missions had us flying in the following countries; Germany, Rumania, Italy, France, Czechoslovakia, Yugoslavia, Greece, Hungary and Austria.

In the case of my crew, we got split up very early after we arrived. The first day in combat, our radio man was assigned to another plane, shot down and became a prisoner of war. Our ball turret man was wounded over Ploesti Romania within the first two weeks of combat missions. The right waist gunner was killed over Austria. The tail gunner had a nervous breakdown, went AWOL and was court martialed. Our pilot developed hepatitis and was hospitalized. Our bombardier became very proficient and was moved to headquarters, to fly a lead ship.

As for me, I was lucky. Not a scratch.

B-24 Nose Gunner

Arthur Chace

as told to John Reardon
Dec 2015

At 91, "and proud of it," Arthur Chace lives on memory lane. Really, Memory Lane, Frankford, DE. Aptly, as it turns out, for he has memories to tell.

As a B-24 nose gunner in Italy, some of his flights were almost literally seared into his memory. He casually mentions being "distracted" on one mission when two engines were on fire simultaneously. That turned out to be the first of two emergency landings in Yugoslavia, on a field just big enough to land on.

He remembers other missions where the flak was "thick enough to walk on." And others when they collected the shrapnel in the plane after landing, and wondered why no one was hit.

He remembers how quickly a B24 would lose altitude with two engines out, while the "Glory Guys" in B-17's claimed they could easily "press on." (He clearly remembers the contrast in the attention given to the Italian front vs. the "Western" front.)

But at the beginning of the war, he remembers that "they needed everybody." So even though he was a Quaker, with an almost automatic CO status, he signed up as an aviation cadet, while still in high school. He was on active duty shortly after his 1942 graduation, and just before Thanksgiving, 1943, after a year of stateside training, Arthur Chace met his crew at Springfield AAF in Massachuesetts. It was destined to become an excellent crew, and a very lucky one. An early omen of their good luck occurred when they were assigned a brand new B-24 to transport to Europe, just in time for a Thanksgiving dinner in Scotland. This was at a time when most new crews were being sent across a cold north Atlantic on troopships. (The same good fortune reoccurred eighteen months later, when they again escaped the troopships.)

From Scotland, they flew to Marrakech, Morocco, and then on to their new base in Italy. They were to be part of the 15th Air Force, 450th bomb group, out of southern Italy. Upon reporting in, they weren't allowed to keep the new plane, but instead were assigned to a B-24 named "Seldom Available."

After eighteen months, and twenty seven combat missions, the entire crew somehow remained unscathed. They had flown over France, Italy, Germany, Austria, Hungary, Romania and the Balkans. They had flown in the Polestoi oil raids, and "Big Week." They had had in-flight fires and emergency landings and had flown through flak and fighters. They were on missions where 200 planes were lost. They supported ground troops, both American and Russian. They saw friends bailout and others shot down and crash. Somehow, their luck held.

Perhaps their closest call was just prior to their second emergency landing in Yugoslavia. In attempting to cross the mountains, they had to jettison anything they could, in order to lighten the plane and gain altitude.

Chace is very proud of his ten man crew, three of whom still survive. He said they could always trust their pilot, greatly admired their navigator, thought the bombardier was "strange," and were absolutely devoted to each other. With gunners at nose, tail, top, bottom and both sides, they totally relied on each other. In particular, they admired the ball gunner, who, once in position, had no way to exit without their help. There was never any friction or shirking. Despite many close calls, no one ever dropped out or claimed illness.

But Chace still reserved his highest praise for Francis Heroy, his navigator, a former math teacher. "It was very comforting how he "read the stars" and brought us across the Atlantic, and right over." However, he was soon taken from them and assigned to lead nav. Then after five missions, he arranged for the entire crew to join him.

Arriving in Italy when they did meant that they would be in combat for all of 1944, through VE day in 1945. Twenty seven missions. Eighteen months. Twelve hour missions.

He is amused to remember both the living arrangements and the daily drill of those flying days. They lived six men to a tent – canvas covered, cement blocked walls. Cold muddy winters. Long, hot summers. In the elements. Close quarters. Particularly close on that day when a tentmate suddenly disrupted the quiet with an accidental discharge of his pistol. He also chuckles to remember that there were very few promotions. "No money available," they were told.

Daily assignments appeared on the bulletin board. Five AM would bring alert, breakfast, briefing, preflights, takeoff, ammo testing, circling into formation, going on O2, and then the long, long lookout for enemy fighters.

The bomb run, the flak, the damage, and hopefully the return, a shot of whiskey, and the debrief.

After a long year of combat flying, Arthur Chace knows right where he was when he learned that President Roosevelt had died. He was in flight, returning from a twelve hour mission.

He cannot say where he was on VE day, but he knows where he was on VJ day – He was getting married. In fact, the entire summer of 1945 was a very fast blur:

The European war had ended, and he had returned home for B29 training in Florida, in preparation for the remaining war with Japan. He became engaged, married, and rather quickly discharged.

Soon after VJ day, when all additional B29 training was canceled, Chace, with his 27 missions was among those eligible for a quick discharge, "if he wanted it." He WANTED it. He was told he could report to Indiantown Gap, PA for discharge. It was a fast summer.

It was quite a contrast to 1944!

B-24

Arthur Chace

Arthur Chace

Pilot Training - Joseph J. Pearce
Contributed by Vernell Abella   Dec 2015

Joe enlisted in the Army Air Corps at Scott Airfield, Illinois, on December 18, 1941.   He attended radio operators school at Scott Field from Jan–Jun 1942. He applied for Aviation Cadet Training and after an extensive screening process, was accepted on September 12, 1942, to "Preflight Instruction." This was mostly hazing, designed to eliminate individuals who lacked the stamina, or desire required to make it through flight training.

Joe started "Primary Flight School" at Decatur, Alabama (Oct –Dec, 1942.) He flew a PT-17 (Stearman) which is an open cockpit biplane. Primary was 10 weeks long and emphasis was on stalls, spins, takeoffs and landings, eventually flying solo.   The final phase of Primary consisted of advanced aerobatic maneuvers, and cadets were liberally "washed out" for any perceived weakness from air sickness and flying skills to "military bearing."

The next school he attended was "Basic Flight Training," at Walnut Ridge Arkansas.   This was a ten week school flying BT13A which was a more advanced airplane. Emphasis was on cross country flight planning, navigation, aerobatics, instrument and formation flying.

After Basic, he was transferred to Freeman Army Airfield, Seymour, Indiana, where he started "Advanced Flight Training," and flew an AT-10 (twin engine bomber.) Joe graduated on November 3, 1943, receiving his aeronautical rating and a commission as a Second Lieutenant.

He was then transferred to Hendricks Field, Florida where he began training in the B-17 bomber, more commonly known as the "Flying Fortress" (based on its ability to keep flying after sustaining considerable damage, and also for its heavy armament - 50 caliber machine guns.)

After completing B-17 school, he was transferred to MacDill AAF, Florida where his crew met for the first time. They received training in combat tactics, formation flying, navigation, bombing and aerial gunnery, with emphasis on working together as an integrated crew.

After completion of combat training, Joe and his crew ferried a B-17 across the Atlantic Ocean to Ridgewell Airdrome in England, home of the 381st Bomb Group. They received more training in combat tactics and on June 22, 1944 they were assigned "Combat Status." They began flying combat missions as a crew on June 25, 1944. Joe and his crew flew a very intense schedule during the month of July and August. In the month of July he flew 14 combat missions and an additional 7 days of flight training. They flew together less and less as different crewmembers were randomly assigned to other crews as replacements.

Initially, Joe was required to fly 25 missions, and the chaplain had told him that the average survival rate was 15 missions. Upon returning from his 23rd mission, he was informed that a new policy had been established, requiring 30 missions. Then, just prior to completion of his 30th mission, the requirement had again been changed - to 35.

Joe flew his 35th and final mission with his ball turret gunner, Robert ("Shorty") Harper. After landing and taxiing to their assigned parking spot, he asked Shorty to come up to the cockpit – honoring him by saying, "Shorty, shut these engines down." Joe had survived 35 combat missions and departed Ridgewell January 2, 1945 at the young age of 24.

On The Home Front During WWII

Viola C. Willey 1995 by Holly Smith
Contributed by Vernell Abella   Dec 2015

My maternal grandparents were married in 1941. Even then, Europe was in a troubled state, and young men here were having to sign up for the draft. They knew they would no doubt be called into service. But December 7, 1941 still slipped up on America. In a sneak attack, the Japanese attacked Pearl Harbor. Many lives were lost, many wounded, and many ships sunk.

My grandparents tell me most of the people in their age group remember vividly just where they were and what they were doing when the news came over the radio. This was before TV, but radios were in use in homes and many, but not all cars. This changed life in America drastically, and permanently for many.

However, almost without exception, the families of those called into service, and those already in service, had a strong feeling of patriotism. This generation said the Lords's Prayer and the Pledge of Allegiance before school classes would start. Everyone either saluted or held their hand over their heart when the Pledge was said or the Star Spangled Banner was played. Even though loved ones left home, it was with a feeling of pride that men, and some women (the WACs,) left for duty. And the ones left behind in tears still had that feeling of pride. There were some draft dodgers, but in no way could the feeling be compared to the feeling later about the Viet Nam war.

It has been said that 1940 was probably one of the happiest in the lives of American people. The parents of my grandparents lived though the depression in the late 1920's and the early 1930's. My grandparents were really too young to remember those early years, though in the poorer families many did remember the struggle their parents went through. This would be felt at Christmas when many children had to settle for a stocking with some fruit and nuts and maybe just one or two little toys. Children of the poorer families remember this well.

There were a lot of homes that still did not have refrigerators until after WWII. The ice-man came around daily, making his stops, leaving ice at many homes. Of course, the more prosperous did have refrigerators in the 1930s. The milkman also made regular stops at homes every day, including Sundays. Because of the war, many products weren't available, even to people with money. My grandmother well remembers that "old wooden stroller." She hated it. Everyone could hear her coming and going. This was 1943, and metal strollers weren't to be found anywhere, so she had to settle for a wooden one to push my uncle in. She well remembers their icebox, too. She always had to remember the drip pan underneath, or there would be a spill over.

It was a lonely time for many, especially for parents with only sons. Everyone who had someone in the service hung a flag about 5"x7" in the window with stars denoting how many in their immediate family were serving, A death would bring a flag with a gold star instead of blue.

My grandmom had a flag with two blue stars – one for my granddad and one for her brother. My grandparents first child was born in1943 but still it was a very lonesome time. Grandmom didn't work and the days and evenings were often very long. After putting her son to bed she would always write granddad a letter. She joined a book club and the highlight of her days was the mail man bringing a letter from my granddad or a new book. The government allotted her $80 a month (one child.)

Granddad saved many of his letters from grandmom, and she saved his. They are in their cellar today all packed into an old army duffle bag. They say someday they are going to bring them up and spend an evening reminiscing. (My granddad served in the 98th Bomb group of the Army Air Corps, as an armorer with an outstanding B-24 Bomber group of the 15th Air Force in Italy, which chalked up over 300 missions. Their group had been awarded two Presidential citations and a score of commendations for its participation in bombing attacks on every important objective in Europe.) Grandmom kept a scrapbook of clippings, some Italian paper money, whatever granddad sent home. The clippings are now yellowing and fragile, but still intact.

The young women who didn't have children worked, saving for the day when their husbands came home and they could set up housekeeping or buy a lot or a new car. A lakefront lot could be bought for $500 after the war and lots in town were $150 and up. Also, many were looking forward to buying refrigerators and washers when they became available after the war. Washers had been available before the war but some of the really poor people were still using a scrubbing board.

One of my grandparents friends recently published a little booklet. She had been raised and still lives in Rehoboth Beach, the leading resort in little Delaware. In her booklet "A Study of Old Rehoboth," Ann Lynch tells some of what our parents and grandparents experienced in the war years:

"During the war, we had a little discomfort. Oh, gasoline and tires were rationed, and you were only permitted to drive 35 miles per hour. Sugar and butter were also rationed. This was the beginning of margarine as we know it today. It was called oleo, and came in a bag with a yellow capsule enclosed which grandmother kneaded until it turned yellow. Shoes were also rationed, and unavailable. Silk stockings were replaced with rayon stockings and rayon underwear. They were so ugly, and I can't believe manufacturers are using rayon again for women's clothing. It must be less expensive than other fabrics.

"Our parents were instructed that the top half of their automobile headlights must be painted black and their draperies must be closed when lights were on inside the house. This was so no aircraft could use the lights as targets. The boardwalk did not escape this edict. The businesses had to black out their windows and the lights on the boardwalk were not turned on. And it was DARK out there. However we still had people walking the boardwalk.

"US Seaman were on patrol each night through morning on horseback up and down the beach and there was a curfew. We felt well protected by Fort Miles near Cape Henlopen. It was manned mostly by our soldiers of the army. Many concrete towers were erected along our coastline and several can still be seen today.

"Certain days of each week the sound of shells bursting during air target practice could be heard well into the town of Rehoboth. Enemy submarines were sighted off our shores and the Town of Lewes and Beebe Hospital saw many foreign sailors who suffered mishaps or were ill and brought to their facilities to treatment. This was another era in our small town history."

My grandparents especially enjoyed this section of Mrs. Dyer's booklet. It brought back many memories. Granddad's father wanted to "do his bit for the war effort" and he was an Air Raid Warden. He was issued a white hard hat, an armband, and a strap for over his shoulder. One of his duties was to patrol the streets to make sure the homes had darkened their windows, and headlight tops were painted, etc. In Milford, where my family lived, every home was instructed to have sand and water stored in the basement.

May 8, 1945, was V-E Day, (Victory in Europe,) and Sept. 2, 1945, was V-J Day. Grandmom especially recalls May 8 vividly. Everyone knew the war was coming to an end. Word spread around Milford in the early afternoon, and for several hours without letup, people seemed to go wild. Everyone was out on the sidewalks, or riding around in cars, honking horns, windows down and shouting out the windows as they went by. Every church in town rang and rang their bells. Grandmom remembers too, the sound of the ambulance. One of the neighbors, who had lost her son in the war, had a heart attack and had to be taken to the hospital. It was a day of joy and tears. She says it was a day that she will always remember.

This meant granddad would soon be coming home. He was home on a short furlough that summer and on Sept 8, 1945, he was discharged. They soon found a double house, -- rent $17 a month, and bought a full size, three piece living room wicker set for $15. They lived about a block from his parents and they were lucky enough to have use of his parents' car.

Almost immediately after the war, many new things that people wanted started appearing on the market. Many women who had been working wanted to continue to work so they could have more material things, and it seems they have worked ever since. Before the war, with exceptions, of course, mothers just didn't work. Few families had more than one car. Very few high school students drove to school. It was the school bus or walk.

One of the first luxury products that appeared after the war was TV. It didn't seem like too many years before practically every family had a TV. The first ones were black and white and often snowy, but we all thought it was great anyway. Color wasn't too long following black and white, but was very expensive. Most made out with black and white until prices started to come down. The first color sets, though expensive, had snow, but that didn't bother anyone. We all considered TV some sort of a miracle.

Young couples were advised to wait on buying a home – prices would come down, they were assured. NOT TRUE! Every year prices continued to rise and never did go down. My grandparents bought their first home in 1950. Government loans at low interest rates were available to veterans, and this helped many a young couple to buy their first home.

This was an era that brought many changes and many new inventions and has continued ever since. The quiet family life seems to be a thing of the past. My grandparents believe there is a lot more stress for everyone, even for the younger people, but it is something we have to learn to live with since it seems there can be no turning back.

88th Infantry Division

S. SGT. ARNOLD PIERSON

Blue Devils

SSGT Arnold Pierson

E Co, 2nd Battalion, 251st Reg, 88 ID, 5th Army
As Told to John Reardon
Dec 2015

"Yes. I was involved in the war. Very involved, and I brought home a souvenir to prove it." With that, Arnold Pierson 95, uncovers his left forearm. There is a nasty scar where shrapnel entered near his elbow, and a visible lump inside the elbow, where it became lodged. It remains there, a source of amusement at airports and other places with devices unable to distinguish a 95 year old from a terrorist.

He remembers being hit during an artillery barrage, just as he crouched into his foxhole. (Five years later, as a tourist, he was able to revisit the scene and located his foxhole, complete with remnants of his C-ration containers.)

At the time of the injury, he was just patched up, packed with sulfa powder, purple heart recorded, and back to the job. "It was just a scratch compared to what was happening to others." But it was an honest wound, compared to some "self inflicted" cases he saw, where desperate soldiers just wanted out, at any price.

But, to start at the beginning. At 21 on Pearl Harbor Day, Pierson knew his life was about to change. He was soon drafted, but was allowed to finish his last semester of college before reporting to Fort Dix, N.J. After his final stateside training, he remembers the relief they all felt when they saw they were headed east, and not west to the Pacific.

They were soon on a Liberty ship, attending classes between bouts with sea sickness. After a few days of adjustment, they were more concerned with several sub scares, and lifeboat drills. He also remembers the beauty of the heavens at midnight once the ship was away from all lights.

First stop was in North Africa. It was the first time he saw mules and donkeys, and found it interesting that the men would ride, while the women walked. (Mules and donkeys became common place once they were in Italy, but no one rode – they carried ammunition.)

From Africa, Pierson's unit was among those sent to relieve the Anzio and Salerno beachheads, where our forces were trapped. After the initial landings, the enemy held the high ground and was able to zero in on beach, ships and planes. Some thought they would be driven back to the sea. Pierson said he knew a lot of prayers, and said them often. He remembers how the more senior veterans always seemed to be soaking their feet! The cold and wet were taking their toll.

After the beach head, in mid 1943, Arnold remained in Italy, under fire off and on, for nearly two years. At one point they were in combat for 100 consecutive days. It was a long, drawn out campaign, taking them over many mountains, rivers, villages and defensive lines – The Hitler line, the Gothic line, the Siegfried line, the Apian Way, the Po Valley. He remained with the Fifth Army, advancing through Italy until the war ended.

His photograph album brings back many random memories:

Bivouacing in the Appenines

Apennine Bivouac Area
December, 1944

15

REST AREA—The above picture of Mark Luther, taking a bath in an irrigation ditch, and Fred Clayton, sitting on the bank. The photo was taken in Italy, 1944 in a rear rest area prior to the assault on the Gothic Line.

Bathing when and where you could – a roadside ditch or a city fountain.

In one rear area, there was even time to invite the local beauties to a dance and buffet:

Siete gentilmente invitata a partecipare alla nostra

Serata Danzante

con buffet, sabato 2 giugno alle ore 20 alla Filarmonica - Via Verdi N. 30

Co. E. 2nD. Bn 351 Inf.

STRETTAMENTE PERSONALE

Pierson's primary duty was to maintain communications. There were radios, phone lines, maps, walkie talkies, and battery back packs. There was placement, recovery and repair. But mostly it was the footsoldier's long walk through the hills of Italy. It could be a cold, wet country. And there are many isolated memories.

He remembers an instance when they were marching in two columns, one on each side of a road. The German soldier approaching them on a motorcycle was as surprised as they were to discover his mistake. In the confusion, he had time to turn around and make a hasty retreat.

Then there was the time in the remote mountains when Pierson became separated from his unit for nearly a week. His parents actually received an MIA notice. He "walked a lot," and survived on whatever rations he carried, until he found the lines again. Communications weren't very good at that point.

One young "gung ho" lieutenant once ordered a ridiculous "fixed bayonets" charge to take a town. "It wasn't WWI. It was useless, and we came upon one dead German."

Pierson modestly says he "fired often," but never knew the results. No close combat. He is still amazed at how fast you can dig a foxhole while flat on your stomach. He entered Rome (after a year's fight) just as the Germans were leaving at the other end, arguably among the first to enter Rome.

In Rome, Arnold Pierson was one of about twenty who were selected for an audience with Pope Pius XII. The Pope said, in English, that he wanted to thank some American soldiers for not bombing Rome. He gave them his blessing, and a brief visit.

This brush with the famous reminded Pierson that back in the states, he had also once been selected - two men per company - to "have lunch" with President Roosevelt. "He came into our barracks, leaning on his son's arm, and spoke to us beforehand."

Yet another contact with a celebrity occurred right on the front lines. Arnold had once written about it:

"It was late afternoon, May 11, 1944. I was in a tunnel-like hole that I had dug into the side of an embankment. That night, as soon as it was dark, E company would move into position and wait until 11:00. Then, from one coast of Italy to the other, thousands of guns, including ships at sea, would open fire on German positions, and we would begin to attack the Gustav line.

Waiting is always the hard part. So I was glad when I was told that I was wanted at the Co. CP. There, I was introduced to a middle-aged man in uniform, whose name was Frederick Faust. He had written western stories under the pen name of Max Brand. He wrote on many subjects, under many different pen names. He was well known everywhere. He wrote poetry, movie scripts, and even the "Dr. Kildare" series, later made popular on TV. I shook his hand, said that I was glad to meet him, and went back to my foxhole, and my thoughts.

He was there to be part of our infantry attack, as a war correspondent. He didn't have to be there. He must have known that people would die that night. Several days later, I found out that he had been killed shortly after the attack started. There would have been a lot for him to write about had he lived. I lived. But he could have told the story of that night so much better."

Arnold Pierson had also written about **Monte Cassino:**

"2/27/44 - 3/3/44
"In those seven days, I became aware of what it would mean to be a combat infantry soldier, and a lot of it would be about fear; about realizing for the first time that I could be killed. Until that time, it was just doing what you had to do to make it as a soldier. Now, there was a new dimension: being ready to kill, and trying not to be killed. Monte Cassino was to be the first of a number of gut testing experiences.

"Before going there, I knew very little about the Abbey of Monte Cassino. While in North Africa, I read about the attempt of the US 36th Division to cross the Rapido River and capture the town of Cassino. The attempt was a disastrous failure. Some of the officers of the 88th including General Kendall, CO of the Division were present as observers. Some were wounded, and it became clear that capturing Cassino would be difficult and costly. Overlooking the valley was the Abbey of Monte Cassino. From there, the whole approach to Cassino could be observed. The Germans claimed they were not using the abbey for that purpose, but they were not believed.

"In early February of 1944, the Second Battalion of the 88th Division (E Company was part of the Battalion) was moved to an area near Cassino. I watched wave after wave of allied medium and heavy bombers pass over on their way to bomb the Abbey of Monte Cassino. In the distance, we could hear the sound of exploding bombs.

"Soon we went by truck to San Michele. There, in a rock quarry, on a hilltop, we waited until dark. In front of us and down below us, was a battery of artillery firing toward the German positions. When it became dark enough, we

left the quarry, and wound down to Rte 66, the road that would lead to Rome if we could get past Cassino.

"It was not so dark that we could not see the destruction all around us. It reminded me of pictures I had seen of World War I: Shattered trees, shell holes, and destroyed vehicles. We walked single file to the Rapido River, and there moved upstream to where a bridge had been constructed, crossed the bridge, and began climbing a rocky foot path up the steep hill in front of us. Going up, and coming down, were men leading mules. In the dark, I could not see what they were carrying - ammo, rations, water, or bodies. As we climbed, shells, were bursting on the ridgeline above us. It was not easy going.

"It was, or had been raining, and the path was slippery. We were going to relieve elements of the 36th Division, who sent guides to lead us to the positions we were to occupy. They had dug foxholes and one was chosen to be E Co command post. I found a hole nearby. It was not very deep because the area was very rocky. But rocks had been piled all around its top and it was covered with a "shelter half." (canvas tent section.) So it was dry, and lined with parkas and blankets. It was a bit of luck, because it was in the dark, and I had found a wonderful foxhole. Of course, when shells are falling any hole is a wonderful hole. The next day, we must have been seen by the Germans as we moved around, because that night and for some nights afterward, the area would be shelled. When the first shells landed nearby, I tried to make myself as small as possible in my hole. I did pray that I be given a little more time. "Please Lord, not now." In the seven days we were there, the Battalion lost 19 men. I still remember the voice of someone after a shelling, in the middle of the night, calling for a medic.

"We were relieved by Indian troops. Then we walked out in knee deep mud at night, back to where we had started. But I was a different person now. I had been where men were killed, and I wasn't. It was great to be alive. The next day, I saw in the distance the ruins of Abbey Monte Cassino for the first time.

In other random comments Pierson recalled hillbilly accents, a wheeler/dealer mess sergeant, who kept them well fed, and a commandeered house they soon abandoned because of the bedbugs.

He remembers his DI Sgt Billows, who "made a soldier out of me," his M1 garand weapon; the "Blue Devils" nickname they received from Axis Sally; and the award received from from the "Prince of Piedmont, General of the Realm."

No. 2559

He remembers being greeted in some villages with bottles of wine. Wine that some soldiers drank like soda pop (with predictable results.) (There were times when the most dangerous thing in Italy was a drunken American soldier.)

Well after Rome, the pursuit continued. He remembers feeling the bullet whiz past, when he was shot at by a sniper. The position was quickly identified, but the sniper had made a fast getaway. They crossed river after river on rubber rafts and Duks. They wrote many Vmails home, but never received enough back.

After the surrender, Pierson's unit was assigned to transport German POW's back to Germany. One armed GI was assigned to each train car. No trouble was expected. They were going home too. Before the return trips, there were "tourist" opportunities. He visited Hitler's stronghold at Berchtesgaden, and actually stood on the balcony that Hitler had used.

ALLIED FORCES

A P. IN MIDDLE
FNDING

After VE day, expecting to be heading for Japan, Pierson declined an OCS offer for the second time, and glad he did. Lieutenants had a high mortality rate.

Overall, he's proud of his service – he did his job the best he could, made friends, and survived his three and a half years in the war.

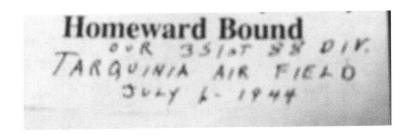

Homeward Bound
OuR 35/st 88 Div.
TARQUINIA AIR FIELD
July 6 - 1944

"They will live a long time, these men of [WW II.] They had an American quality. They, like their victories, will be remembered as long as our generation lives. After that, like the men of the Confederacy, they will become strangers. Longer and longer shadows will obscure them, until their Guadalcanal sounds distant on the ears, like Shiloh and Valley Forge."

James A. Michener

Appendix

Contributors to "A Soldier, A Sailor..."

In order of appearance

Joe Carter   "Bloody Hatten."

Contributed by Fran Brumbaugh, who found it after seventy years.

Rank: Captain

Branch: Army

Unit: :   47th Tank Battalion, 14th Armored Division.

Duty: Tanker

Inducted:

Discharged:

Theatre: France, Belgium, Germany

Awards n Decorations:, EAME ribbon, Victory Medal

Summary: Nordwind, at Hatten, Last German Offensive

Quote: "Behind were the fires, and the dead; Behind was the broken offensive."

Bob Clancy

Rehobth Beach DE
Navy Seabee.
Contributes the Navy portion of his memoirs.

Rank: Carpenter's Mate, 2nd class

Branch: Sea Bees

Unit: 82nd Construction Btn

Duty: Building Airfields

Inducted: 1/27/43

Discharged: 1/18/46

Theatre: South Pacific, Solomons, Mariannas

Awards n Decorations: Asiatic Paciic, with four stars,

        American theatre, Victory Medal

Summary: Island hopping, building airfields

Quote: " Can Do."

"I became grateful for blessings that were previously taken for granted."

Bill Stratton

Elinor Stratton   Seventeen year old warbride, relays her husbands stories from Pearl to Iwo Jima.

Rank: Corporal

Branch: USMC

Unit: Third Marines

Duty: Infantry

Inducted: April, 1941

Discharged:

Theatre: Pearl Harbor, Iwo Jima, Guam, Tokyo

Awards n Decorations:

Summary: A Pearl Harbor, and Iwo Jima survivor came full circle, and walked the land of his former enemy.

Quote: Millions of lives were saved by the A Bomb, and after Okinawa, it was clear that the Japanese wouldn't have surrendered otherwise

Bob Austin

Bob Austin   Veteran of two USMC amphibious landings
Happily tells his story "in living color."

Rank   Tech Sergeant

Branch   USMC

Inducted   December, 1942

Discharged December 1945

Theatre   Pacific

Awards n Decorations:, Asiatic Pacific, Victory Medal

Summary: Veteran of landings at Saipan and Tinian.

Quote: "But the assault waves had landed on bloody
beach Blue Two."

Clifford Chronister

A close look at a crewmember's daily life.

Rank   SSgt

Branch   Army Air Corps

Inducted

Discharged

Theatre   Italy

Awards n Decorations:

Summary: 's daily life.

Quote: "As planes were shot down, another bunk would be empty for a while.."

Arthur Chace

Arthur Chace   Tells of his time as a "Nose gunner."

Rank: S Sgt
Branch: Atrmy Air Corps, Nose Gunner
Inducted   June, 1942
Discharged: Sept. 1945
Theatre: Italy
Awards n Decorations:
Summary   Twenty seven B-24 combat missions out of
Italy.
Quote: "Flak was thick enough to walk on."

Joe Pearce

Joe Pearce   Outlines his pilot training in detail, and only casually refers to his 35 combat missions.

Rank: Lieutenant

Branch: Army Air Corps

Duty: B-17 Pilot, England

Inducted: December, 1941

Discharged:

Theatre: European

Awards n Decorations: .

Quote: After 35 missions: "Shorty, shut these engines down."

Viola C. Willey

Viola C. Willey   Describes life on the homefront in Milford DE. to her grand daughter

Rank: Soldier's Wife

Branch: Homefront

Unit: Letter writing

Duty: Keep the homefires burning

Inducted: 1942

Discharged: 1945

Theatre: Stateside, Milford De

Awards n Decorations: Two blue stars in window

Summary: Describes life on the homefront in Milford DE. to her grand daughter

Quote: "It was a lonely time."

88th Infantry Division

Arnold Pierson

Arnold Pierson   Infantryman for two years in Italian campaign.   Told his story in the month preceding his passing.

Rank: SSgt

Branch   U. S. Army

Unit: 88th Infantry

Duty: Communications

Inducted: June, 1942

Discharged: 1945

Theatre: Italy

Awards n Decorations: PH, EAME, , Victory Medal

Quote: "I had been where men were killed, and I wasn't.."

"Like many other American men my age, I have always admired – nay, stood in awe of – the G.I.s. I thought that what they had done was beyond praise. I still do. To get to know so well a few of them has been a privilege."

Stephen E. Ambrose

"Everyone has a story to tell. All you have to do is write it.

But it's not that easy."   Frank McCourt

Do you have a veteran's story that should be preserved?

Please contact me at   John13cav@comcast.net

Books by John T. Reardon

Our World War II Heroes

More World War II Heroes

Still More World War II Heroes

A Soldier, A Sailor, and a Marine
   Walked into this War

19 in '44

You Almost Got Used to It

Anything Could Happen Next,
   Take Care of Your Friends

A Civil War Cavalryman, Our Ancestor

Remembrance,   with Shirley Olsen

My Year in Vietnam,   with Barry Popkin

OUR WWII HEROES

MORE WWII HEROES

STILL MORE WW II HEROES

19 in '44

A SOLDIER A SAILOR AND A MARINE

YOU ALMOST GOT USED TO IT

John T. Reardon, Lt. Col, (ret) USAFR, served as a C-5 navigator at DAFB. After he published his first book about his great grandfather's adventures in the Civil War, his readers contributed more first person veterans' accounts, requesting that they also be preserved.

He has now interviewed over fifty "eye witnesses to WW II," and written ten books. He pays tribute to all veterans by preserving these accounts so that a younger generation may have a glimpse into the experiences of the "Greatest Generation."

$15 ea + $2 postage   <u>John13cav@comcast.net</u>   302-242-1827

145